D0884712

FLOODS

by Lois Sepahban

Content Consultant
Stephen A. Nelson
Associate Professor of Geology
Tulane University

CORE
LIBRARY

Published by ABDO Publishing Company, PO Box 398166, Minneapolis, MN 55439. Copyright © 2014 by Abdo Consulting Group, Inc. International copyrights reserved in all countries. No part of this book may be reproduced in any form without written permission from the publisher. The Core Library™ is a trademark and logo of ABDO Publishing Company.

Printed in the United States of America,
North Mankato, Minnesota
052013
092013
♻ THIS BOOK CONTAINS AT LEAST 10% RECYCLED MATERIALS.

Editor: Lauren Coss
Series Designer: Becky Daum

Library of Congress Control Number: 2013932180

Cataloging-in-Publication Data
Sepahban, Lois.
 Floods / Lois Sepahban.
   p. cm. -- (Earth in action)
ISBN 978-1-61783-938-2 (lib. bdg.)
ISBN 978-1-62403-003-1 (pbk.)
1. Floods--Juvenile literature. 2. Natural disasters--Juvenile literature. I. Title.
551.48--dc23

                          2013932180

Photo Credits: Shutterstock Images, cover, 1, 28, 32, 45; Stock Montage/ Getty Images, 4; Red Line Editorial, 9, 41; AP Images, 10; Thinkstock, 12, 14; C. A. Carrigan/Shutterstock Images, 16; Dave Martin/AP Images, 18; Jack Schiffer/Shutterstock Images, 20; Shabina Lourdes Dalidd/ Shutterstock Images, 23; Bob Jordan/AP Images, 26; Andres Leighton/AP Images, 31; Czarek Sokolowski/AP Images, 34; Tim Merrick/US Geological Survey, 36, 39

CONTENTS

FRANK LESLIE'S

ILLUSTRATED

JOHNSTOWN

NEWSPAPER

Entered according to Act of Congress, in the year 1889, by the JUDGE PUBLISHING COMPANY, in the Office of the Librarian of Congress at Washington.—Entered at the Post-office, New York, N. Y., as Second-class Matter.

No. 1760.—VOL. LXVIII.]   NEW YORK—FOR THE WEEK ENDING JUNE 8, 1889.   [PRICE, 10 CENTS. $4.00

CHAPTER ONE

THE JOHNSTOWN FLOOD

Floods were a fact of life for the residents of Johnstown, Pennsylvania. Johnstown is located in a river valley. It sits where the Little Conemaugh and Stoney Creek Rivers merge to form the Conemaugh River. Like many areas in western Pennsylvania, this river valley is a flood zone. The rain began falling on May 30, 1889, and didn't let up. It was clear that Johnstown would be flooded again.

The 1889 flood of Johnstown, Pennsylvania, was the worst flood the United States had ever experienced.

The Great Storm of 1889

The May 30 rains were part of what became known as the Great Storm of 1889. Early on May 31, the streets of Johnstown were under two to seven feet (0.6–2.1 m) of water.

Conemaugh Lake sat 14 miles (22.5 km) upstream from Johnstown. After a night of nonstop rain, Conemaugh Lake was ready to overflow. The ground around it was soaked from all the excess water. Neither the lake nor the ground could hold any more liquid. But the water kept rising.

The Dam Breaks

The South Fork Dam stood between Conemaugh Lake and Johnstown. The dam was 35 years old. And it needed repairs. Water began spilling over the top of the dam shortly before 3:00 p.m. on May 31. Within moments the center of the dam broke. A wall of water rushed down the Little Conemaugh River at 40 miles per hour (64 km/h). The wall of water measured

35 to 40 feet (11–12 m) high. The deluge was ready to destroy anything in its path.

The Great Wave

Within minutes the wall of water crashed into the village of South Fork. Most residents there had listened to the dam officials' warning. Many South Fork residents had evacuated. Even so, four people died. Thirty homes were destroyed.

Approximately 40 minutes later, the flood hit Mineral Point. There 16 people died. Next, the flood destroyed the railroad yard in East Conemaugh. Thirty-seven

Dams

People have been building dams across rivers since before 3000 BCE. Dams control the flow of rivers. Dams are used to change the direction of rivers. These structures can store water used to water crops. Dams can also create man-made lakes for fishing and boating. Like many dams of the 1800s, the South Fork Dam was made of packed earth. Earth and clay dams break fairly easily. Modern dams are made of concrete and steel. These dams are stronger and better able to withstand the water increase brought on by heavy rains.

train passengers disappeared in the flood. Woodvale was the next village in the path of destruction. More than 300 people died there.

One hour after the South Fork Dam broke, a giant wave of water and debris was headed straight for Johnstown. At 4:07 p.m. the flood hit Johnstown.

Missed Warnings

On the morning of May 31, officials in charge of the South Fork Dam realized it was in danger of overflowing. They sent a messenger to South Fork, the village just below the dam, to telegraph Johnstown of the danger. The warnings either never arrived or they were ignored.

The Stone Bridge

The flood took ten minutes to race through Johnstown. Thousands of people drowned or were killed by debris. As the flood rushed through Johnstown, it hit a railway bridge called the Stone Bridge. The bridge survived the force of the wave. But the floodwater was filled with debris. A wall of train

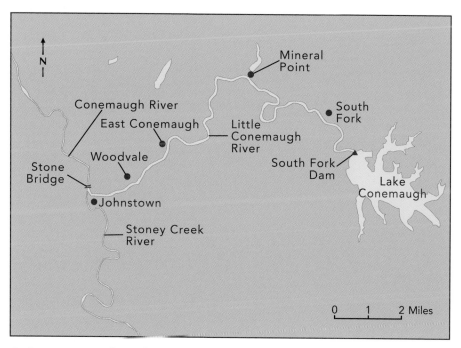

Johnstown Flood Map

Use this map to trace the path of the Johnstown Flood. The distance from the South Fork Dam to Johnstown is approximately 14 miles (22 km). What did you imagine the path of the flood looked like when you read about it? How is this map similar to what you imagined? How is it different?

cars, building wreckage, and barbed wire 40 feet (12 m) high was trapped at the Stone Bridge. This mass of debris soon caught fire.

The fire destroyed what was left of the town and took even more lives. The flood and the fire left death and destruction in their wake. In all, 2,209 people died, including 99 entire families. Approximately

A flood survivor stands by a home destroyed in the Johnstown Flood.

1,600 homes were destroyed. Johnstown had been nearly wiped off the face of the earth.

Floods can bring death and destruction. But they can also bring fertile soil and much-needed water to farmland. Floods represent nearly one-third of all of the natural disasters in the world each year. Flood-warning systems have improved since 1889. But floods still kill as many people as hurricanes, tornadoes, and lightning combined.

Clara Barton founded the American Red Cross in 1881 to help those in need. Barton brought in the American Red Cross to help Johnstown Flood survivors. She wrote about what she saw in Johnstown in her autobiography:

> *I shall never lose the memory of my first walk on the day of our arrival—the walking in mud, the climbing over broken engines, cars, heaps of iron rollers, broken timbers, wrecks of houses; bent railway tracks tangled with piles of iron wire; among the bands of workmen, squads of military, and getting around the bodies of dead animals, and often people being borne away;—the smoldering fires and drizzling rain—all for the purpose of officially announcing to the commanding general (for the place was under martial law) that the Red Cross had arrived on the field.*

Source: Clara Barton. The Red Cross in Peace and War. Washington, DC: American National Red Cross, 1906. Print. 158–159.

Consider Your Audience

Read this passage carefully. Barton wrote this description of Johnstown for an adult audience. How would you adapt the text for a younger audience? Write a journal entry describing Johnstown after the flood for young children. How does your new description differ from the original text, and why?

CHAPTER TWO

HOW FLOODS HAPPEN

Floods have one basic ingredient—water. Many different natural and man-made events can trigger the excess of water that leads to a flood.

Soggy Soil

Floods occur when extra water is added to ground that cannot soak it up. Healthy soil acts like a sponge. It soaks up water until it is completely saturated, or

Floods can have many different causes.

Water that can't be absorbed by fully saturated soil will pool on top of it.

filled with water. The ground is unable to soak up more water once it is saturated.

Sometimes, very dry soil is unable to soak up water. This often happens in the western United States. Sometimes a short burst of heavy rain pours into desert soil. If the water comes too quickly, the hard, dry dirt cannot absorb it. A flood may occur.

Winter-Weather Floods

Heavier-than-normal snowfall in the winter can cause spring flooding. As the snowpack begins to melt in the spring, water rushes into the watershed. After a winter with heavy snow, river and reservoir levels in the watershed are high. The watershed cannot handle the extra water. Rivers and streams overflow.

Fortunately, this kind of overflow is predictable. Residents in flood zones are warned when there is a good chance of spring flooding. They may have time to take safety precautions, such as surrounding their homes in sandbags to block

Watersheds

A watershed is an area of land that drains rainfall. Watersheds work a little like a funnel. On the top, the funnel is wide. But it narrows to a much smaller hole. This is how a watershed works. Rainfall covers a wide area of land. That water drains into streams and creeks. The streams and creeks drain into rivers. And the rivers empty into lakes and oceans.

An ice jam occurs when chunks of ice build up on a river.

the water. They may also have time to move their possessions to higher ground.

Ice jams can also cause flooding. These occur when warm spring weather causes the snowpack to melt very quickly. The frozen layer of ice on lakes or rivers can break into large chunks. These chunks block the normal flow of water. The area upstream of the blocked river may flood. Ice jams usually happen slowly. This gives people who live in the flood zone enough time to protect themselves and their belongings.

Failure of Dams and Levees

Dam and levee failures can be much more dangerous than other types of floods. Levees and dams control the flow of water. Dams are built to use the water. They are often used to create hydroelectric power. Levees are built to protect an area from flooding.

Modern flood-warning systems help

Urbanization

People often make changes to the environment that can increase flooding risk. They build dams and levees, towns, and roads. Towns and roads cover the ground with pavement. That means there is less soil to soak up extra water. There are also fewer trees and shrubs to slow the water as it runs down hills and mountains. This water enters lakes and rivers more quickly than it otherwise would. Adding storm drains to streets can reduce flooding in urbanized areas.

After Hurricane Katrina in 2005, parts of New Orleans, Louisiana, flooded when the city's levees failed.

officials evacuate areas in danger of dam and levee breaks. This saves many lives. But some people ignore the warnings or don't get them in time.

Regular inspections of dams and levees can help prevent them from failing. The Army Corps of Engineers recommends that dams and levees be inspected at least once a year. Then any necessary repairs can be made before the next flood. But

EXPLORE ONLINE

Chapter Two discusses watersheds. The Web site at the link below has more information about watersheds. It also discusses the impact people have on their environment. As you know, every source is different. How is the information given on the Web site different from the information in this chapter? What information is the same? How do the two sources present information differently? What can you learn from the Web site?

Watersheds
www.mycorelibrary.com/floods

even dams and levees that are well maintained can fail. Anyone who lives near a dam or levee or other flood zone should have a plan in place in case of an emergency.

CHAPTER THREE

TYPES OF FLOODS

While there are many causes of flooding, there are three basic types of floods: flash floods, river floods, and coastal floods.

Flash Floods

A flash flood occurs when the water level rises too quickly for the soil to absorb the water. Flash floods are most likely to happen near streams or rivers. Areas with a higher volume of man-made construction are

All floods can cause property damage and loss of life.

Flood Categories

The National Weather Service classifies floods into four categories to show how strong they are:

- **Minor flooding:** residents must take safety precautions; no property is damaged.
- **Moderate flooding:** some people must evacuate to higher ground; some properties and roads flood.
- **Major flooding:** many people must evacuate to higher ground; roads and properties are damaged due to flooding.
- **Record flooding:** damage to roads and property is greater than an area has ever experienced before.

more at risk for flooding than areas with a higher volume of soil.

There are many causes of flash floods. Dam and levee breaks or breaches can cause these floods. Heavy rainfall sometimes causes flash floods. These flood triggers can occur many miles from the site of the worst flood damage. Canyons, streams, and channels can fill with water very quickly because water runs into them faster than it can run out. These areas may flood many miles from the actual rainstorm. Ice jams can also cause flash floods.

Flash floods can occur in areas that are normally very dry, such as Arizona.

Because flash floods happen so quickly, they can be difficult to predict. Officials may issue a flash flood warning when a slow-moving storm releases high levels of rainfall over an area. Several storms in the same location may also lead to flash flood warnings.

Flash floods are the most dangerous type of flood because they come on so quickly. People who learn of a flash flood warning in their area should move to high ground as soon as possible.

River Floods

River flooding occurs when the water level in an existing river rises more than the river can handle. Many river floods occur in the same locations every year. These kinds of river floods are predictable. They create floodplains, or level land that is often covered by water.

River floods can be caused by heavy rainfall, tropical storms, ice jams, and melting snow. However, not all river floods are predictable. In 1999 rainfall from Hurricane Floyd caused river flooding in North Carolina. Meteorologists, scientists who study weather, expected the storm to hit Florida. But the hurricane changed direction. People in North Carolina only had about 24 hours to get ready for the storm. Most of the 57 people who died in the storm were killed in the flooding.

Coastal Floods

Coastal floods occur when the ocean water floods onto normally dry coastal land. Sometimes high winds drive huge waves onto shore, causing flooding. Unusually high tides can also trigger major flooding. Coastal flooding is often caused by other natural disasters. During a hurricane, strong winds push water toward the front of the storm. This causes the water to rise when it reaches land. This rise in sea level is called a storm surge. The water from a storm surge rushes inland. The storm surge also rushes up streams and rivers, preventing them from draining into the ocean like they normally would.

Coastal flooding can also be triggered by a tsunami. A tsunami is a series of huge waves caused by an underwater disturbance, such as an

100-Year Floods

Flood scientists use probability, or chance, to give us an idea of how often really big floods happen. The river flooding from Hurricane Floyd was known as a 100-year flood. This means a flood of this size in this area occurs on average once every 100 years. A ten-year flood occurs on average once every ten years. A 500-year flood occurs once every 500 years.

A North Carolina man carries his dog through the floodwaters caused by Hurricane Floyd's rain and storm surge.

undersea earthquake. When these huge waves reach shore, they can cause deadly flooding. In 2004 an earthquake caused a giant tsunami in Indonesia. More than 225,000 people were killed in the flooding caused by the enormous waves.

Floods can be both life-giving and life-taking. Flood survivors often have to deal with the loss of loved ones or personal belongings. Andy Cavenaugh, a North Carolina flood survivor, recalled his experience after the Hurricane Floyd flood:

> *The whole thing brings out the good and bad in people. This gentleman gave me fifty dollars right out of his pocket. Told me I needed it. And I don't even know who he was. Asked me was that my house. I was sitting in there, in the house. I come out. This was before people stole anything. I said yes, this is my house, or what was my house. And he said, "Here, you need this more than I do." "And I said, Man, I don't . . ." and he said, "You take it." So, the whole situation brings out the good and the bad.*
>
> Source: Charles D. Thompson. "'Those Hands': Floyd Flood Survivors and Disaster Assistance." NC Crossroads 5.1 (January/February 2001). Web. Accessed March 12, 2013. PDF. 5.

What's the Big Idea?

Take a close look at this passage. What is Cavenaugh trying to say about being a flood survivor? Pick out two details he uses to make his point. What do you notice about the first and last sentences?

FLOOD ZONES

Floods affect more people each year than any other natural disaster. Floods may be more likely in rainy or wet seasons. But they can happen in any place at any time.

North American Floods

In the United States, more people die in floods each year than in any other natural disaster. Floods are most likely in low areas along streams and rivers.

Around the world, floods cause death, loss of property, loss of drinking water, and loss of agriculture.

Superstorm Sandy

In October 2012, a huge storm called Superstorm Sandy traveled north up the Atlantic Coast of the United States. The areas that received the most snow and rain were in West Virginia, North Carolina, and Virginia However, storm surges along the coast caused floods. The flooding from Superstorm Sandy's storm surge damaged or destroyed more than 100,000 homes and businesses in New Jersey and New York.

Coastal areas are also at risk for floods because of hurricanes and other tropical storms.

In 1900 a hurricane in the Gulf of Mexico caused flooding in Galveston, Texas. That flood killed 8,000 people, making it the worst natural disaster in US history.

Floods in South America

From 1975 to 2000, the majority of flood-related deaths in the world were in South America. However, many of these deaths weren't caused directly by the floods. In 1999 nonstop rain in Venezuela brought heavy flooding. The extra water caused mudflows on Venezuela's hills and mountains.

Between 10,000 and 30,000 people died in the mudflows the flooding caused in Venezuela in 1999.

Asia and Oceania

More people are affected by river flooding in Asia than in any other region. Many rivers in Southeast Asia flood during the rainy season, from summer to fall. These yearly floods can be helpful for farmers. Rivers such as the Mekong in Cambodia or the Brahmaputra in India bring silt to the farmland when they overflow. Silt is nutrient-rich soil. The added silt helps farmers grow healthy crops year after year.

Rice is grown in many parts of Asia and requires great amounts of water to grow. Farmers intentionally flood rice fields.

At the same time, Asian river floods can bring hardship. If the flooding is too great, it will drown the farmers' crops. Many people live on floodplains in Asia. When rivers overflow, floods can destroy villages and towns in their paths.

Flooding is also common in Oceania. This region of the world includes Australia and the islands near

Australia. Heavy rains during the summer rainy season cause flooding in this region every year.

Africa

Most major floods in Africa are river floods. At 4,132 miles (6,650 km) long, the Nile River is the longest river in the world. It starts in Lake Victoria and flows north through ten countries. The yearly floods of the Nile usually reach their peak in late summer and fall. The floods can be very beneficial for farmers. But they can also cause loss of property and loss of life.

In 2012 the Nile River floods were so bad that

Life-Giving Floods

Every summer, the Nile River waters quickly rise as snow melts in the mountains around Lake Victoria. The river floods and brings fertile soil to the surrounding land. For thousands of years, farmers on the Nile River floodplain planted their crops after the floodwaters left. The silt left by the flood helped them grow healthy crops. People even celebrated the annual floods. Today, the Nile River no longer floods regularly in Egypt and many other areas. Modern dams, such as the Aswan Dam in Egypt, now help control the flooding.

In 2010 heavy rainfall in Poland and other central European countries caused massive floods that forced thousands of people to leave their homes.

they destroyed all of the crops. Flood survivors had to worry about finding shelter. They also had to worry about whether or not there would be enough food for the next year.

Europe

Many parts of Europe are also prone to flooding. Scientists working for the European Union are

FURTHER EVIDENCE

Chapter Four describes areas where floods often occur.
If you could pick out the main point of the chapter,
what would it be? What are some pieces of evidence
that support this point? Visit the link at the Web site
below. Find one quote from the Web site that relates to
Chapter Four's main point. Does the quote support an
existing piece of evidence in the chapter? Or does it
add a new one?

Floods around the World
www.mycorelibrary.com/floods

concerned that climate change could increase

Europe's flood risk. As the earth's average

temperature is increasing, it is causing ice trapped at

the earth's North and South Poles to melt. Scientists

believe this melting will raise the sea level. Coastal

regions may be more likely to flood due to higher

sea levels.

CHAPTER FIVE

FLOOD SCIENCE

Scientists go to great lengths to better understand floods. They try to understand how past floods occurred. Scientists hope this will help them predict future floods more accurately. They also study weather patterns and forecasts to learn where floods are most likely to occur.

Two US Geological Survey (USGS) workers install equipment to help monitor river flooding in Idaho.

El Niño

El Niño is a weather pattern that begins in the Pacific Ocean. It begins when the ocean water near the equator is warmer than normal. That causes more rain in the southern United States and parts of South and Central America. The extra rain brings flooding to those areas.

Studying Floods

Precipitation forecasts are predictions about how much rainfall can be expected in a particular area. Scientists pay close attention to these forecasts. When more rainfall than normal is expected, scientists are able to issue a flood watch. This means flooding might occur. Scientists issue flood warnings when a flood is actually occurring or is almost certain to occur.

Flood mapping is another tool scientists use to predict floods. To make a flood map, scientists look at the history of flooding in a particular location. They use aerial photographs and satellite images of floods in that area. The scientists can compare these images to see how the area flooded in different years.

Scientists can compare two photos of North Dakota's Little Missouri River flooding from 1972, *top*, and 2011, *bottom*, to make predictions about how the river might flood in the future.

Flood Control

Today people around the world build structures to help prevent and reduce flooding. Engineers design and build levees to keep water from rivers and oceans from spilling over onto dry land. Seawalls are built along coasts to help protect cities and roads from coastal flooding.

Turn Around, Don't Drown!

Many flood-related deaths occur in cars. Drivers think their cars or trucks can make it across flooded roadways. But it only takes six inches (15 cm) of water for most drivers to lose control of their vehicle. The National Weather Service put together a safety campaign to help prevent flood-related deaths. The campaign is called Turn Around, Don't Drown.

Architects and engineers design flood-resistant buildings that are more likely to survive a flood. These buildings are made of materials less likely to become damaged if they are under water for a long period of time. In some places prone to flooding, governments require homeowners to purchase flood insurance. In places with a severe flood risk, the governments may offer to buy houses from people who live in flood zones. Then these people can move to safer places.

Scientists are hard at work trying to accurately prevent and predict floods. Early warning of floods can save lives and property. Scientists want to know

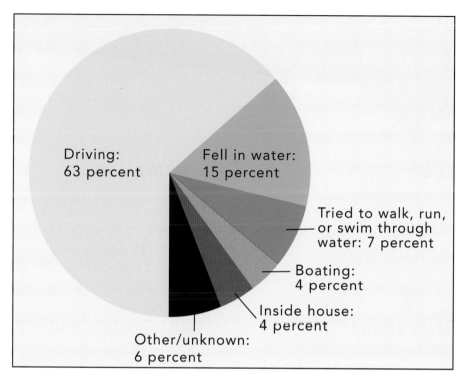

Driving: 63 percent

Fell in water: 15 percent

Tried to walk, run, or swim through water: 7 percent

Boating: 4 percent

Inside house: 4 percent

Other/unknown: 6 percent

Flood Fatalities

This chart shows the US flood deaths in 2011 and how they occurred. You have read about the National Weather Service's work in flood education and flood safety. How does the information in this graph change the way you will behave during a flood? How will you be better prepared to act in the event of a flood?

where floods will happen, when they will happen, and how severe they will be. Modern flood prediction and warning systems save many lives every year. Floods will always happen. But with these tools, scientists hope to limit the death and destruction floods cause.

TEN MASSIVE FLOODS

1099
The Netherlands and England
More than 100,000 people were killed when unusually high tides flooded the Thames River in England and low-lying areas of the Netherlands.

May 1889
Johnstown, Pennsylvania
This flood and the fire that followed completely wiped out the town of Johnstown, killing more than 2,000 people.

September 1900
Galveston, Texas
On September 8, a Category 4 hurricane swept through Galveston. The storm surge flooded the city's streets, leaving more than 8,000 people dead. It was the worst natural disaster in US history.

April–May 1927
Mississippi River
Known as the Great Mississippi Flood of 1927, this flood covered 26,000 square miles (67,300 sq km) across Illinois, Missouri, Kentucky, Tennessee, Arkansas, Mississippi, and Louisiana. Approximately 500 people were killed and 600,000 were left homeless.

August 1931
China
The Yellow River is known for its frequent flooding. The 1931 flood covered 42,000 square miles (109,000 sq km). It may have killed as many as 4 million people directly and indirectly over the next several months. It left more than 80,000 homeless. It was the highest number of fatalities caused by a flood in recorded history.

August 1954
Iran

A storm with unusually heavy rains led to massive flooding across Iran. More than 10,000 people were killed in the disaster.

August 1971
Vietnam

Approximately 100,000 people were killed when the Red River flooded. Because the flood took place during the Vietnam War (1954–1975), scientists don't know much about this disaster.

December 2004
Indian Ocean

An earthquake caused an enormous tsunami that devastated Indonesia and other nearby countries. More than 225,000 people were killed in the flooding.

August 2005
New Orleans, Louisiana

When Hurricane Katrina struck the US Gulf Coast, the storm surge caused levees to break outside of New Orleans, sending water rushing into the city. More than 1,800 people were killed in the storm, many as a result of flooding.

July–November 2011
Thailand

In the summer and fall heavy rains led to severe flooding across Thailand. The floods killed more than 600 people and wiped out more than one-fourth of the country's rice crop. More than two-thirds of the country was covered in water at some point during the floods.

Why Do I Care?

The Johnstown Flood happened more than 100 years ago. But that doesn't mean you can't find similarities between your life and the world of the Johnstown Flood survivors. How does the Johnstown Flood affect your life today? Are there safety precautions that might not exist without it? How might your life be different if the Johnstown Flood had never happened? Use your imagination!

Take a Stand

After the Johnstown Flood, many survivors blamed the group responsible for the South Fork Dam's maintenance for its failure. Many tried to sue the group, but the lawsuit failed because the flood was considered a natural disaster. Do you think the victims should have won their lawsuits? Or was the court right? Write a short essay explaining your opinion. Make sure to give reasons for your opinion, and facts and details that support those reasons.

Say What?

Studying floods means learning a lot of new vocabulary. Find five words in this book that you've never heard before. Use a dictionary to find out what they mean. Then write the meanings in your own words, and use each word in a new sentence.

Tell the Tale

Chapter Four of this book discusses the 1999 Venezuela flood. Write 200 words that tell the story of the mudflows and floods there. Describe the sights and sounds flood victims might have seen and heard. Be sure to set the scene, develop a sequence of events, and offer a conclusion.

GLOSSARY

debris
the remains of something
broken down or destroyed

deluge
an overflowing of the land by
water

evacuate
to leave a place because it is
dangerous

floodplain
level land that is often
submerged by floodwaters

levee
a bank built along a river to
prevent flooding

meteorologist
a scientist who deals with the
atmosphere, weather, and
weather forecasting

reservoir
an artificial lake where water
is collected and stored
for use

saturated
to be so full of water that no
more water can be soaked up

silt
very small particles of
sediment from water

snowpack
seasonal accumulation of
slow-melting packed snow

watershed
an area of land that drains
rainfall

LEARN MORE

Books

Bailey, Rachel. *Superstorm Sandy*. Minneapolis: ABDO, 2014.

Eagen, Rachel. *Flood and Monsoon Alert!* New York: Crabtree, 2011.

Koponen, Libby. *Floods*. New York: Scholastic, 2009.

Web Links

To learn more about floods, visit ABDO Publishing Company online at **www.abdopublishing.com**. Web sites about floods are featured on our Book Links page. These links are routinely monitored and updated to provide the most current information available.

Visit **www.mycorelibrary.com** for free additional tools for teachers and students.

INDEX

ABOUT THE AUTHOR

Lois Sepahban has taught every grade from kindergarten to high school. In her free time, she reads books, writes stories, and rescues animals.